God Rest Ye Stressed Communicators

Planning Christmas for Your Church

Edited by
Edited by Elizabyth Ladwig & Kevin D. Hendricks

ISBN-13: 978-1517405380
ISBN-10: 1517405386

Published by the Center for Church Communication
Los Angeles, California
www.CFCCLabs.org

Copyright © 2015 Center for Church Communication

Cover design by Sheri Felipe.
Print layout by 374 Designs.

All rights reserved. No part of this book may be used or reproduced in any manner whatsoever without permission, except in the case of brief quotations.

Let nothing you dismay.

Contents

Foreword by Stephen Brewster

Planning

Practical Planning
by Katy Dunigan

Embrace Tradition for Your Christmas Celebration
by Kevin D. Hendricks

The Geography of Christmas
by Dave Shrein

Think Inside Your Box
by Evan Courtney

Advent: Don't Reinvent Christmas
by Kevin D. Hendricks

Christmas on Purpose
by Kelley Hartnett

Killing the Christmas Pageant
by Darrell Vesterfelt

A Church Lover's Christmas Service Tour
by DJ Chuang

Promotion

8 Ways You Can Promote Your Christmas Series Or Event
by Evan Courtney

10 Ways Your Church Can Have A Social Media Christmas
by Paul Prins

Christmas Communication Lessons From Last Year
by Karen Shay-Kubiak

13 Last Minute Christmas Ideas
by Robert Carnes

Welcoming Visitors During & After Christmas
by Jonathan Malm

Over-Christmased

The Treason of the Season: Stop the Stress
by Kevin D. Hendricks

Hospitalized by Christmas
by Anne Marie Miller

For the Love of God, Rethink Christmas
by Josh Cody

More

About the Center for Church Communication

More Church Communication Help

Social Media Graphics

Acknowledgements

Foreword

by Stephen Brewster

I love Christmas. The memories, the music, the smells, the weather—but most of all, I love the anticipation. There are few other times in the year that build to a climax the way Christmas does. For example, everyone engages. It doesn't matter the age, gender, race, creed, color—everyone. It's so much fun. It's also a natural time for the church to step into the conversation. It's one of a handful of holidays built around a principle of Christianity, the birth of Jesus. We get to be inserted right into the dead middle of the conversation, the epicenter of all the anticipation!

So what do we do with that opportunity? We try to plan efficiently, but often we get buried by all that is happening in our churches and our personal lives. We get overwhelmed by fears of not marketing our Christmas traditions well enough to draw people in. We need ideas.

What if we had a resource available to us to help us make our Christmas more impactful? I think that is what this team has done with this Christmas book—they've created a tool to help our churches better share the joy of Christmas.

I love how Darrell talks about his time in the church and how their team came up with the Christmas for the City parties. That is such a killer idea. Putting on a party helps people see our churches as relevant beyond Sunday and part of our real lives. This party helped their team create a new, affordable, inclusive tradition for people. I wish I had known about this information when we started A Merry Music City event at Cross Point two years ago. I would have called Darrell to find out what his team had learned. Creating new traditions that incorporate old traditions is an easy way to develop momentum and energy for your church.

Communication during Christmas is really hard! There are so many messages just dominating people's attention. Karen Shay-Kubiak is great at communicating and is systematic about breaking through the noise. Her article about how Elmbrook essentially doubled their attendance at Christmas was so encouraging to me as a person responsible for the attention and promotion of Christmas services! I loved that they were able to not only target, but also attract people to their community who are not associated with any faith community. Really, this is living out their mission during one of the busiest times of the year. Brilliant and so purposeful!

How the Grinch Stole Christmas is one of my absolute favorite movies. I have a feeling that my guy Josh Cody is a fan as well. Joshua is so good at challenging people to think differently. Yes, Christmas is a time of tradition, but it is also a moment for artists and creative people to dig in and reimagine what could be said, done or experienced. After I read his chapter on reimagining Christmas, I felt ready to go become a change agent! Josh is inspiring.

And that's just three examples of the lessons this book offers. No matter where you're at, Christmas is an opportunity for you, your church and your team. As you read this book, my prayer is that you are challenged, inspired, educated and moved. Not just moved to go to work, but moved to find your place in the holiday season in your community. God has a plan for you and for your church. He is going to give you ideas and opportunities to impact your city, provide hope for people who need it and help ramp up the anticipation of not just opening presents on Christmas morning, but celebrating the grace and hope that the season was built on. (And this grace and hope lasts a lot longer than a new sweater or fruitcake.)

This is your moment. A chance every year to spread the news of Jesus Christ coming to earth as a tiny baby, wrapped in swaddling clothes and lying in a manger. As communicators, we have the privilege of bringing good tidings of great joy for all people…

"For unto you is born this day in the city of David a Saviour, which is Christ the Lord." (Luke 2:11 KJV)

Merry Christmas.

Stephen Brewster has the honor of serving as the creative arts pastor at Cross Point Church in Nashville, Tenn., and served for the past 15 years in professional creative environments including church, music business, marketing, management, artist development, creative team leading and art directing. He lives in Franklin, Tenn., with his wife Jackie and their amazing kids.

Web: StephenBrewster.me
Twitter: @B_rewster

Planning

Practical Planning

by Katy Dunigan

The holidays are a special time of celebration and joy for most people, but for church staff, the holidays can also be a time of increased stress and pressure. Whether it's a Christmas Eve Service, Christmas Day Mass or a New Year's Praise Service, there are many planning details to remember and arrange leading up to the special event. Some details can be managed ahead of time and some details must wait until the day of, but careful, intentional planning ensures your holiday service is successful and deeply meaningful.

Here are some basic planning tips to help you prepare:

1. Pray

Begin as soon as you are given the assignment. Prayer is the key to success. Ask God to guide you in your planning and preparations. Ask him to help everyone involved in the event. Ask him to bless your service and the people who attend.

2. Start Early

Begin a minimum of eight weeks in advance. Early preparation is vitally important. Eight weeks might seem early, but it isn't. Meet with your church staff to design the service's theme and tone. You can move forward in your planning once those details have been decided.

3. Communication

Start advertising a minimum of six weeks in advance. If you want to share the good news with a lot of people, you must ensure they hear about your service every week leading up to it. It's important to communicate this to potential visitors in several different ways:

- **Website:** Post the event clearly on your website with the specific details such as the date, time, location and some photos of last year's holiday service.
- **Social Media:** Post the event on all of your social media platforms, and post regularly. Facebook, Twitter, Instagram, Pinterest—whatever platforms you utilize, make sure the information is out there for your members and potential visitors to see. You can create a communication plan and also ask volunteers to help spread the word.
- **Snail Mail:** Yes, people still use the postal system, and a print invite might be happily received by your church neighbors. Consider mailing a postcard invitation—just be sure to mail it at least three weeks in advance.
- **Email:** It's a very popular way to communicate, but be sure the service announcement doesn't get lost in the clutter. Don't just send

the announcement in the church e-bulletin. Email it separately to make it stand out and gain special attention.
- **Church Sign:** God's message isn't outdated, and your church sign shouldn't be either. Post the worship service details on your church's information sign, and as soon as the service is over, remove it and post new information.

4. Childcare

Begin coordinating with childcare staff eight weeks in advance. Childcare is a very important element to include in your planning, as it often determines whether or not families with young children can attend the service. The types of childcare available should be communicated when announcing the service. This ensures your members and guests can plan accordingly.

5. Decorating

Begin planning a minimum of eight weeks in advance. Planning the service involves decorating for it, and the holidays are a busy time. Put a decorating team together early, develop a decorating theme and get started as soon as possible. Make sure the decorating coordinates with the theme and tone of the worship service.

6. Logistics

Begin planning a minimum of four weeks in advance. It's a special holiday service, and your church, sanctuary, gathering area and parking lot will be packed with people! Exciting—but challenging. Here are the main factors you need to be concerned with:

- **Parking:** Recruit volunteers to help with parking and traffic. Consider asking your volunteers and regular attendees to carpool in order to save parking spaces for guests. If you live in a cold and snowy climate, make sure you arrange for the parking lot to be cleared of snow or ice before the service.
- **Hospitality:** Recruit volunteers to greet and guide visitors. A warm "Hello, we're glad you're here" will go a long way in connecting with new faces. Make sure your volunteers are well informed, can answer guests' questions and can guide them where they need to go.
- **Signs:** Check your signs. Do they clearly communicate where the nursery is located or where the bathrooms can be found? Think like a visitor, and plan accordingly!
- **Food:** Are you providing light snacks before or after the service? Make sure you provide more than enough food and drinks so you don't run out and people aren't left feeling awkward and not included. Jesus could feed a crowd of people with a miracle, but you can't.

- **Seating:** Know your seating limits in advance, and make an "overflow" contingency plan. Set up television monitors for the overflow area so attendees can both hear and see the service. Decorate the overflow area so it feels comfortable and connected with the primary worship area. Also, make sure the seats in the overflow room are arranged prior to the worship service. Making people stand and wait for a seat in an unattractive room isn't cool or comfortable.

7. Support Your Participants

Begin planning at least three weeks in advance. Whether it's the lead pastor, the nursery workers, worship singers or greeters, your service participants need your support. They will be giving of themselves, their time and their talent. Perhaps you're offering multiple services in one evening or just one big service. Either way, support your staff and volunteers.

If you're offering multiple services in a row, set up a "green room"—a place participants can go to relax, eat a little snack and experience fellowship with fellow participants. If it's just one service, plan a post-service get-together where everyone can gather to celebrate the service's success and you can express your appreciation for them.

You might consider catering a small meal. That

will need to be arranged a few weeks ahead of time. Sometimes you can find volunteers in your church willing to provide the food. If that's the case, awesome!

8. Last-Minute Preparations

On the day of the service, communicate the event on social media and via email. It's important to remind everyone and encourage them to come.

Also, remember the practical planning items:

- Sit down and pray. Spend time quietly reflecting on God's peace, and ask for his presence before, during and after the service. Believe in him to work in the hearts of those attending and participating in the service. Thank him for what he's doing and will do.
- Check the thermostat to make sure it's set at a comfortable temperature. Remember that a lot of people will be in the room. Don't set the temperature too high.
- Check the bathrooms to make sure they are clean and well stocked.
- Clear the welcome area of any trash and clutter.
- Light candles early to create a pleasant aroma and atmosphere.

9. Follow-Up

Once the service is over, you may feel exhilarated or exhausted, maybe both. It's important for you to take time to recover.

Within a week, send thank you notes to your participants. A handwritten note is always appreciated. Take the time to write them.

Within two weeks, sit down with your participants to review the event. Highlight what went well, and discuss any problems encountered during the event. Discuss and explore ways you can improve on both the positives and the problems. This will help in planning the next big service, which is most likely just around the corner.

Although many details go into planning a large service or special event, the end result is worth the effort. The opportunity to share the life-changing message of God's love, peace and hope is absolutely amazing. Believe and rely on him as you plan each big and small event throughout the year. Remember you are doing more than managing details—you're making a way for people to find and know Christ, and that's the most important detail of all.

Katy Dunigan is the marketing and social media director for OnlineChurchDirectory.com and serves on Indiana's SW District UMC Leadership Team. She is also active in the digital #chsocm community and is a Center for Church Communication Street Team member.

Twitter: @KDunigan

"Christmas is filled with opportunity. You can pull off some amazing things because people's hearts are already there."

Gary Molander
co-owner
Floodgate Productions

Embrace Tradition for Your Christmas Celebration

by Kevin D. Hendricks

Here's some quick advice for your Christmas celebration: **Embrace tradition.**

No matter how contemporary and cutting edge we may be, **at Christmastime people like tradition.** There's a reason we sing the same Christmas songs, bake the same cookies and trot out the same old box of Christmas decorations every year. There's room for an innovation here or there, a new song, a new arrangement, a new cookie. But not much room. People like the classics. It's why Coke rolls out the glass bottles and the Norman Rockwell Santa Claus.

So roll with it.

When it comes to Christmas, people like "That's how we've always done it" just fine.

So don't "put baby Jesus on a zip line." Stick with tradition.

Christmas Traditions to Embrace

As you're thinking Christmas, think traditional. Don't reinvent the wheel.

- You can't get more traditional than the Christmas story. What are the two greatest moments in *A Charlie Brown Christmas*? His sad little Christmas tree and Linus reading from the Gospel of Luke. There's a reason they went simple and traditional. It's powerful.
- Go for classic Christmas songs. That's what people want to hear, and that's what they want to sing. A new song is OK, but keep the ratio heavily slanted to the classics.
- Nothing is more traditional than a candlelight service. Break out the candles, dim the lights and sing some "Silent Night."
- Advent is pretty traditional, too. We'll cover it in a later chapter.

You can build your service around these traditions. You can also work these traditions into your communication. Use classic imagery in your social media posts, announcement slides or postcards.

Tweaking Tradition is OK

Now don't take this as advice that everything has to be boring. **If you're making tradition boring, you're doing it wrong.** Tradition is powerful—it taps something deep within us.

What are some of the top Christmas movies? *It's a Wonderful Life* and *Miracle on 34th Street*. You can't get more traditional than that.

But you can play with tradition a bit. Some of the other top Christmas movies focus on tradition but also play with it a bit. From *Elf* to *Scrooged* to *Christmas Vacation*, it works. Even *A Christmas Story*, which practically wallows in traditional, also pokes fun at it. The movie is a little over the top and romanticized. That was very intentional.

Nearly every TV show that does a Christmas special touches on tradition in some way. They draw on tradition (because it's what people want), and then find a way to tweak it and make it work in the context of their show.

So it's OK to play with tradition. You don't have to play it straight. You can do "Silent Night" with candles and then break out glow sticks and take it up a notch. (Well, maybe in some churches you can do that. But don't try it in mine.)

However you do it, find ways this Christmas to embrace traditions in your church.

Good News for Small Churches

More than anything, embracing tradition at Christmas is **good news for small churches**. If you don't have a huge budget or if you've got a small team and limited resources, embracing tradition is your friend. It means you don't have to come up with some brilliant, brand-new strategy that completely re-imagines Christmas. You don't need something wild to get people's attention. They're eager to pay attention. They're yearning for the traditions they remember. All you have to do is find ways to tap into those traditions.

Kevin D. Hendricks is the editor of Church Marketing Sucks and editorial director for the Center for Church Communication. He's a freelance writer and editor in St. Paul, Minn., and likes to read a lot—he wrote *137 Books in One Year: How to Fall in Love With Reading*.

Web: KevinDHendricks.com
Twitter: @KevinHendricks

"We start having Christmas meetings in July. We'll theme our office around Christmas— we'll hang decorations, we'll turn the air on really cold, we'll have hot chocolate, play music, and really set the mood and the atmosphere."

Stephen Brewster
creative arts pastor
Cross Point Church

The Geography of Christmas

by Dave Shrein

In the event you are not aware of this, Phoenix has only two seasons: hot and awesome. I often compare living in the Valley of the Sun to living on the West Coast at a fraction of the cost. Though our weather is beautiful right now, there is a hard truth that Christmas never feels like it's supposed to feel. While the rest of the country is layering up for the cold outside, we're still wearing shorts and sandals. It's just a different feel than your traditional white Christmas.

When we consider the impact our geographic location has on "doing church," we focus immediately on the demographics: marriage rates, divorce rates, income levels, education levels and so on. There are fewer conversations that explore how different areas of the country (or world for that matter) connect with and experience different seasons.

As I said, in Phoenix we have only two seasons: hot and awesome. While that makes for a goofy one-liner, it highlights the fact that Phoenix doesn't have a true winter. Christmas is one of those times that naturally lends itself to reflection, thankfulness, family time and many other virtues and fruits of the Spirit. It is imperative that we, as church leaders, overcome the limitations of our geography and leverage what makes our culture unique.

The Truth About Phoenix

On Nov. 1, I opened Facebook to find several of my friends had already put up their Christmas trees. Usually this tradition is reserved for Thanksgiving weekend when all Americans join together to "deck the halls." Not in Phoenix. The second those carved pumpkins are trashed, the tree goes up! This speaks to something very unique about my city.

Phoenicians psyche themselves up for Christmas before the rest of the country.

Pumpkin spice lattes and peppermint mochas are on menus much earlier here (though we will drink them iced). Rather than ignoring what's trending in our everyday culture, we need to focus on why this is happening. We Phoenicians want holiday drinks and Christmas sales early to remind ourselves that while we're still in shorts and t-shirts, the rest of the world is chopping firewood for the coming Christmas winter.

My Church's Response

The desire to be reminded that Christmas is coming led us to create a 40-day countdown strategy. During the 40 days leading up to Dec. 25, we used our online platforms to share pictures of one of our students,

Ian, getting ready for Christmas—decorating sugar cookies, buying wrapping paper, hanging stockings, writing to Santa along with 36 other activities. Each image had a stamp on it with our church name and our Christmas Eve celebration times. We shared other related content, but our signature campaign was "Countdown To Christmas."

It was rewarding to walk through our lobby each Sunday and hear our people talking about the daily Christmas pictures. It connected deeply with them because each day they checked Facebook, there was a reminder from Ian: "You better get ready, 'cause Christmas is coming!"

The Truth About Your Location

Geography matters for many reasons beyond pure demographics. If you live in freezing cold temperatures all winter long, what helps residents get through the annoyance of shoveling snow to experiencing the beauty of the season? If your hometown is rainy for hours each day, are there any fun events that happen in the rain every year? Something that could help make that day's rain a bit more sentimental?

This Christmas, make a commitment to use the uniqueness of your geography to help people to experience the reason for the season.

Dave Shrein is the author of The Communicator's List, a free publication for church communicators. He writes about leadership and communications on his blog and is also the host of our Church Marketing Podcast.

Web: DaveShrein.com
Twitter: @DaveShrein

"Create opportunity for engagement. Don't just tell your people what to do. Give them things to interact with. Last year our Advent series was a theme each week—hope, peace, joy and love. On stage we had these big wooden marquee letters spelling out each word. We got the idea to put those words out on the campus just as an extra element. What ended up happening is people wanted to take family pictures and pictures with their friends on these words and share them with their community. So we didn't say, 'Do this.' We just gave them something to experience and engage with, and they did the rest."

Haley Veturis
social media artisan
Saddleback Church

Think Inside Your Box

by Evan Courtney

When Christmas rolls around, creative teams across the globe feel the pressure to "one up" the church next door or even their own previous Christmas worship experiences. There is this pressure and expectation that we have to pull out all the stops and do everything humanly possible to create engaging worship services and "wow" attendees. Just because you can get the latest piece of technology—the snow machine, the flying angel—should you? Should we double and triple our production budgets for Christmas?

When you're planning for Christmas, ask this question: "After our Christmas services, will the people who attended recognize us when they come back next week?" Be sure not to go so far beyond who you are as a church during Christmas that when January comes, nobody recognizes you.

If you came to my home for a special Christmas dinner, we'd go the extra mile. You'd see a blown-up Santa Claus in the front yard, half-lit candy canes illuminating the sidewalk and icicle lights hanging from the roof. You'd walk in, and there'd be "Silver Bells" playing and Christmas dishes on the table with red and green towels that double as napkins at each place setting. But if you came three days after

Christmas, you'd come to a half-shoveled sidewalk and a house overrun with toddler toys and paper plates. You'd be wondering, "What happened to the other house I was at? I must be at the wrong place."

That might be OK at my house, but it doesn't work at church. Sometimes we have that same approach with our services, and we communicate something different than who we really are to those attending services. Visitors come back only to be confused. They may think we have an identity complex or that we set up some sort of facade.

This Christmas, let's think inside our box. Find ways by looking at the skills and resources of your own personal team and the church to be creative and develop engaging worship experiences. When resources are limited, creativity is released. Our most creative experiences come out of the times when we have to think beyond purchasing a piece of equipment or renting gear. It's easy to purchase something, but all we've done is peruse Amazon. The God-given creativity flows out of us when we have to rely on him.

5 Ways To Think Inside Your Box When Creating Christmas Services

1. Decorate Your Exterior

People will interact with your facility before they interact with people. Every church has a tub of

Christmas tree lights. String some lights on your signage. Put a couple of speakers in your parking lot to play a Christmas radio station. Both of these tactics will create a sense of expectation with the resources you already have.

2. Surprise and Delight With Christmas Giveaways

As people exit your worship experience, dress up your guest services teams with Santa hats and give them platters of candy canes to pass out.

3. Organize Shared Experiences

Since you are going to be experiencing higher attendance than normal, use it to your advantage. Get your people involved in an experience together. Find a world record that you can beat during one of your services. Record Setter has numerous ideas for things you can do in a service.

4. Provide Generosity Moments

During the Christmas season, people are in the giving mood. They are looking for a cause to support. Is there something your church can get behind and give toward? Create a project that will develop momentum. This will let first-time guests know you are a church that looks out for the needs of others. Find a local ministry or nonprofit organization you can bless during Christmas.

For example, Cross Point gave a large tip to their bagel delivery guy on a Sunday morning as one of these moments.

5. Build a Sense of Fun and Laughter

At the beginning of your services, engage with your audience. When someone laughs, they become more relaxed and allow God's word to penetrate their heart.

You have to be intentional to pull this off. A couple of ways you can do this is by showing a Christmas video (e.g., a recording of kids talking about Christmas) or playing a stage game.

I'm not talking about youth ministry games with water guns and Pepto Bismol tabs, but think of the kinds of games that Jimmy Fallon creates. These will allow your crowd to loosen up, release the morning stress of getting their kids ready and let them know that church is fun. They'll know it's OK to have a good time. In return, this will help them get involved during worship and connected to the message.

Don't Stop Here

These are just a few things you can do to heighten your worship experience while staying inside your limitations. Don't stop at these suggestions though.

Explore your boundaries, and find something unique and true to your church you can present to your congregation. This will ensure those attending your Christmas services will experience who you truly are the rest of the year.

Evan Courtney is an executive pastor in the middle of the Illinois cornfields at The Fields Church. He owns a creative design company, Creative Courtney, and is a Creative Missions alumni.

Web: EvanCourtney.com
Twitter: @EvanCourtney

"In general, I have a communications strategy where I plug many of the pieces in. I'm always looking for new things to shift without hurting many of the widely loved traditions. I start sometime after Rally Day (usually the last week in September) planning for Advent and leading up to and through the season."

Neal F. Fischer
director of communication
South Carolina Synod of the
Evangelical Lutheran Church in America

Advent: Don't Reinvent Christmas

by Kevin D. Hendricks

Christmas is coming.

It may be a day away, a couple weeks or even a few months, but it's coming, and you need to have a game plan.

Are you panicking yet? Well, don't.

The Perfect Christmas Marketing Campaign

As you're planning Christmas this year, looking for new and better Christmas ideas, trying to figure out how to sing from the mountaintops that Jesus is born, don't panic. **Remember that the church has already created the ultimate Christmas marketing campaign.**

And we did it hundreds of years ago.

It's called Advent.

Rather than devising your own plan and pushing yourself into a crazed, eggnog-fueled stress breakdown, remember Advent.

What's Advent?

It's an age-old build up to Christmas with four weeks of ready-made stories (the prophets, Mary's annunciation, John the Baptist, etc.), stage elements (lighting the Advent candles) and an emphasis on not over-doing Christmas. Honest. Instead of unleashing Christmas immediately after Halloween, churches that are serious about Advent won't even sing Christmas carols until Christmas Eve. Now that's restraint.

Advent is a different kind of lead-up to Christmas, and it's not quite as stressful.

Consider taking your Christmas insanity down a notch this year. Embrace an ancient tradition that ushers in the king with humility and grace instead of an ever-more elaborate spectacle.

Remember the stinky shepherds and a lowly manger? Not a lot of polished entertainment happening there.

Some Advent Ideas

Here are few ways you can incorporate Advent into your Christmas planning:

- Go traditional and do the whole Advent wreath, candle-lighting thing. No need to reinvent the wheel, especially when there's

already a wreath.
- Instead of putting on a massive sermon series leading up to Christmas, just use Advent. Piggy-back on the standard stories each week, and use Advent imagery as your guide to Christmas.
- Rather than brainstorming an angle, go with the whole expectant, waiting—pregnant—idea of Advent. Everything will fit nicely together because that's the whole point of Advent.
- Save your Christmas blowout for Christmas. Hold back on the carols and glitter, and build up the anticipation.

Already on Board With Advent?

If you're already on the Advent train, congrats. The rest of Christendom is playing catchup, but you understand the wonder of the wait.

For the Advent pros out there, please, share your insights with the rest of the neighborhood. **December is such a frenzied month people can be too overwhelmed to even think about going to church.** Let them know that your church is a stress-free zone.

A service of candles and no carols might be just what weary shoppers need come mid-December.

Kevin D. Hendricks is the editor of Church Marketing Sucks and editorial director for the Center for Church Communication. He's a freelance writer and editor in St. Paul, Minn., and likes to read a lot—he wrote *137 Books in One Year: How to Fall in Love With Reading*.

Web: KevinDHendricks.com
Twitter: @KevinHendricks

"I would challenge you as you are planning Christmas to think about what it is that your community needs your church to be."

Chuck Scoggins
creative director
New River Church

Christmas on Purpose

by Kelley Hartnett

Call me Scrooge, but I need to remind us of something: People are losing interest in attending church. And why wouldn't they? Some of the meanest, greediest, judgmental-ist people they know are Christ-followers. Their Christian coworkers aren't any happier or fulfilled than anyone else. The churches in their community are great at telling people how they should live, but they don't see them actually, *ya know, living that way.*

If that's all I knew of church, I wouldn't bother with it either.

But you know what? *I'd probably still go at Christmastime*—because my husband asked me to or because it's what we did with Grandma when I was a kid or because I'm feeling a little lonely or because it's just sort of What We Do, even though I'd hardly consider attending any other time of the year. Unless, of course, I experienced something that caused me to raise my eyebrows and think, "Huh. Well, that's different." So as Christmas approaches, let's think about that reality for a bit.

For me—and for a good percentage of people around me—"different" has almost nothing to do with pageantry and production and almost everything to do with caring for under-resourced people and fighting inequality of all sorts. But I guess that's just me and the kids I play with.

So what about the folks in your community? Who are they? What do they need and want? That's a tough question, I realize, but it's worth investigating—and right now, rather than in December when the machine's already in motion.

Throw out this question at your next planning session: **How can we engage our community in meaningful ways this Christmas season?** After you talk with staff and key leaders, broaden the conversation to include your neighbors, law enforcement, school counselors, government officials, community agencies and so on. **In short: Become an anthropologist in your own community.**

Just to be clear: I'm not hating on Christmas plays and parties and live Nativities and camel rides. Unless, of course, you're deciding to do those things Just Because. If you are, you could be wasting a whole lot of time and energy and financial resources on something your current church family loves but that has your community—the people whom you're hoping to reach this Christmas—rolling their eyes. You want them to raise their eyebrows instead.

Need specific ideas? Here goes:

- If you're in an artsy area, hosting a community art fair or concert series could add value to people's lives and show that you "get" them.
- If you're in an area that's impoverished, set up school supply donation stations around your community and have a stack of invitation cards next to the collection box.
- Charge admission for your event, but donate the proceeds to a well-loved charity.
- Partner with that charity to provide something they need—and invite your community to pitch in.
- Lots of people get the "I want to make a difference" bug during the Christmas season, so help them do that by producing a Random Acts of Christmas Kindness series on Facebook.
- Become known for giving away your Christmas offering.
- Advertise a shortened gathering the weeks before Christmas, after which you'll wrap gifts or make sandwiches for guests at the local homeless shelter.
- Take your Christmas gatherings into your community: subdivision clubhouses, retirement communities and nursing centers, hospital chapels, daycares, etc.
- Discover your community's felt needs, and think of them as key words in your advertising. (Lots of single people? Think con-

nection. Large number of families receiving public assistance? Think hope.)
- Understand your community's perception of "church," and flip that on its head. Surprise them. Delight them.

Know your community. Be creative with that knowledge in mind. And do Christmas on purpose this year.

Kelley Hartnett spent a decade working in established churches and helping to launch new ones. Currently, she's focused on writing, volunteering for organizations that care for vulnerable populations and making progress on her journey toward minimalism.

Web: KelleyHartnett.com
Twitter: @KelleyHartnett

"Don't try to compete with what other churches are doing. Figure out who your audience is, figure out who is showing up at your doors and what's going to reach them. That's what's going to work. … This year, we just scrapped it all. We are not doing a Christmas series."

Neil Greathouse
creative pastor
New Life Church

Killing the Christmas Pageant

by Darrell Vesterfelt

I still remember the Sunday my pastor told us we were canceling the Christmas play. It was 2008, and you could almost feel the tension in the room when he said it. No one understood why he would take something so nostalgic, such a traditional part of our Christmas celebration, and change it.

After all, if it isn't broken, we don't need to fix it, right?

The church loved the traditional Christmas celebration.

The congregation listened to him though because we respected him. We trusted the direction he was taking us, even if we didn't understand it. If we hadn't done that, we would have missed out on something really amazing. That year, Christmas for the City was born.

Christmas for the City

At first, my pastor had a hard time convincing people it was OK to call it a "party." After all, this was a church in the South, and the word "party" had all kinds of negative connotations to go along with it—but that's exactly what it was.

Instead of pouring all of the resources into a Christmas production that meant a lot to our congregation and (frankly) wore out the staff, the church was going to throw a giant celebration for our community.

Everyone was invited—our entire city.

In fact, the vision of Christmas for the City was just as its name describes: It was a Christmas party designed to connect and engage our community. In order to make it a reality, the church had to give up some of our traditional understanding of what a Christmas celebration looked like because it wasn't about us. It was about the city.

No Need to Be Extravagant

The first thing the church had to give up was the idea that Christmas celebrations had to be extravagant.

I'm not sure where we all got this idea, but it seems like every year we felt like we had to outdo ourselves from the year before and outdo everyone around us. This competitive atmosphere, rather than adding value to our Advent season, was stealing our time, energy and resources. And our celebrations weren't necessarily better for it.

Making the transition to simplicity was really

difficult to embrace at first, but once we got over the "need" to outdo each other with decorations or technology, it was actually really freeing.

More Inclusive

We also had to make the celebration more inclusive than it had been in the past.

Most Christmas celebrations look the same. And they aren't the kind of place you want to come if you're not already part of the church community. Since Christmas for the City was a celebration for the city, not for our congregation, the church had to begin to think outside the box about what its new celebration would look like. At first, people weren't convinced, but as they started to connect with other local churches and nonprofits, they began to understand.

On the first year, there were over 6,000 people in attendance. This crazy idea actually worked. It was actually a party for the city.

Now we've added activities for kids, a poetry slam, a story gallery, a "party" room and a live painting area. There is even an area where our nonprofit partners can set up tables and engage with those in the community. They tell their stories, gather volunteers and distribute resources.

It's About Jesus

The church had to make the decision that the celebration was going to be about Jesus, not about the church.

The congregation agreed to get as many other people involved as possible. They asked the local youth choir and symphony if they would like to celebrate with them, and they agreed. They invited other churches to bring their choirs and congregations. Some were reluctant at first, but after a few years, church and community involvement has grown.

Now 35 sponsoring churches, 14 nonprofits and people from over 50 churches participate along with Winston Salem First to put on Christmas for the City in Winston Salem, N.C.

The church's name doesn't appear anywhere on the event. Christmas for the City is not an event hosted by "our church"—it is a nameless, faceless event designed to gather together the capital-C church from all over the community to be the hands and feet of Jesus in the Christmas season. It's a great story.

Sometimes traditions keep us stuck. Sometimes they prevent us from experiencing the kingdom of God right here and now. I'm so glad my pastor had the vision he did and that the church was flexible enough to follow him. I pray you'll do the same this holiday season.

Darrell Vesterfelt is a consultant helping entrepreneurs and bloggers increase their reach and effectiveness online. You can reach him by email at darrell@vesterfelt.com.

Web: DarrellVesterfelt.com
Twitter: @dvest

"Christmas is about messy and surprising and unexpected. God was born in a stable, where a dog probably did sleep in the manger and cows ate their dinner and where a young, scared couple gave birth to their firstborn child, baby Jesus. Nothing perfect about that. And those who came to see him were the ones hanging out that night—shepherds, ninjas, outcasts—whoever heard the angels' invitation and felt joy at being invited. And in the face of baby Jesus, they saw what love looks like.

"Love looks like a teenager texting, an angel in a bad mood and children having fun being in weird costumes. Love looks like our homeless brothers and sisters and those people we call 'enemies.' Love looks like our family and friends, even those who, on this night, we miss because they are with God. Love looks courageous and messy and unusual and simple. Love looks like all of us here tonight.

"The message of Christmas is pretty simple—long ago, on that night, love came down to be with all of us in Jesus. Love... Love came down at Christmas."

Laurie Brock

rector
The Episcopal Church of St. Michael the Archangel (excerpted from "The Dog in the Manger: The Pageant")

A Church Lover's Christmas Service Tour

by DJ Chuang

Christmas is a time for family—both having your family together and being with the family of God. Which is why I have a Christmas tradition of attending as many different Christmas services as possible (our record is 10). I'm happy that my family (wife and 14-year-old son) can enjoy these times with me—I know most people don't enjoy as many church worship services as I do.

But we can never get too much of Christmas!

Christmas Lessons

Attending so many Christmas services gives me a unique perspective. Below are some thoughts on the diversity of celebrations in Christ's church that might be helpful as you're planning your Christmas services:

Christmas has inspired people from all walks of life, not just churches and those who follow Jesus, most obviously through the arts and movies.

We love a wide variety of expressions of worship in different churches.

Churches really do produce their best worship services for Christmas, and that takes a ton of planning, preparation and volunteers.

It also takes a lot of logistical planning to get from one church to the next. I can sympathize with those who go to church for the first time (or rarely) and how being in a strange place not knowing where to go or what to do is quite daunting.

Some of what we saw:

- **Biggest surprise:** Big-band style concert.
- **Most creative production:** Shadow puppets retelling the Christmas story—probably over 1,000 cut pieces and every performance was live.
- **Best Christmas gift:** Family portrait photo shoot.
- **What we didn't see:** A gospel choir, Handel's "Messiah," a Christmas musical cantata, live Nativity with live animals or a drama.
- **Quietest service:** Late night Christmas Eve worship with chapel bells ringing at midnight.
- **No room at the inn:** Nearly half the churches we visited had full-capacity crowds.

To be clear, all of these churches and their Christmas services are not a competition or to be compared; they're a celebration for God's coming as a baby into our midst, and even our mess, and wanting to be with us!

Remember that as you plan and promote your services.

DJ Chuang is a strategy consultant, resource hunter, people connector and ideator. He currently works with the .BIBLE Registry, a new top-level domain for all things Bible, and Leadership Network.

Web: DJChuang.com
Twitter: @DJChuang

Promotion

8 Ways You Can Promote Your Christmas Series or Event

by Evan Courtney

One of the great things about Christmas is that people who don't normally go to church are inclined to go during Christmas if they are asked or given the opportunity to go. We need to leverage this to promote our Christmas series and events so those who are hurting and broken have the opportunity to receive the love of our Savior.

Let's talk about six ways you can get the word out to these people:

1. Mail

Send good ol' mail to both your regular attendees and your community.

Church Mailing List

I know several churches are going away from this, but I still believe a large, nicely designed mail piece (something like 6.5 by 9 inches) increases brand awareness and validity of the professionalism of your church. Send this to everyone on your mailing list. Encourage them to invite their friends.

And even if you feel behind, you still have time to get some postcards printed. GotPrint has a good rush service available.

Direct Mail

USPS has rolled out their Every Door Direct Mail service, which lets you simply enter your address, ZIP code, or city and state for your target areas. They've got a great tool to help you narrow down your audience, which will also help you understand costs.

You could have your pastor write a letter inviting everyone to the Christmas service. It's more personal than a generic event invite and will leave a good impression on those who receive it.

Lumpy Mail

Consider sending lumpy mail. People open lumpy mail. Don't you always open that piece of mail even when you suspect it's junk mail because you know there is something different inside? This could simply be throwing in a small candy cane or something that is branded with the name of your Christmas teaching series.

Here are some ideas of items you could put into an envelope to make it lumpy:

- Balloons
- Invite cards
- Candy
- Pen
- Christmas bow

The people getting this snail mail don't necessarily have to be part of your congregation. Reach out to the people in the community or people who have attended services in the past. The Fields Church in Mattoon, Ill., sent out a mass mailing to anyone who had attended their services in the past five years.

2. Peer To Peer

A majority of people say they attend church because of someone they know. Put a tool in the hands of your attendees to help them invite their family, friends, neighbors and coworkers.

Invite Card

Design a small print piece that you pass out for a couple of weeks before your Christmas teaching series or event starts.

Ideas for invite cards include:

- Business-card sized invite card
- 3-inch round invite card

Home Delivery

Put together a Christmas package that your key leaders can hand-deliver to families in the church, inviting them to your Christmas teaching series or events. This sounds like a lot, but if you have a church of 200, get 20 people to deliver them to 10 families. This would probably only take them an afternoon. If you are larger, just scale those numbers. A church of 2,000 would need to get 200 leaders to deliver to 10 families. Any of your leaders should be able to do this, from ministry leaders, children's workers, small group leaders, pastors, hospitality volunteers, etc.

These are ideas of items for the Christmas packages (include invite cards and promo material with them):

- Christmas cookies
- Christmas candy
- Popcorn

The Fields Church also delivered Christmas Survival boxes to their patrons. Each year they have a theme for their Christmas sermon series, and last year that theme was "Surviving Christmas." They packed each box with items that would help their patrons de-stress:

- Stress ball
- Starbucks coffee
- Candy canes
- Ornaments
- Chocolate chip cookies
- Multiple invite cards
- Coloring pages

Putting together boxes like this one and making home deliveries takes a lot of time and effort, but it helps make a personal connection that can't be achieved through a Facebook or Twitter post.

Caroling Door-to-Door

Christmas carols are a great tradition, but caroling door-to-door doesn't happen very often anymore. Having your church choir go around the neighborhood a few days before Christmas singing Christmas carols is a great way to set your church apart. It'll really get people in the Christmas spirit, and you can even hand out invite cards while you're caroling.

3. Micro-Site

Design a micro-site for your series or event. Develop some good search engine optimization for the site that pinpoints your target audience. Think through keywords your audience may be searching for during the holidays, and make sure those are built into your site.

Keywords that visitors may be searching for are:

- Depression during the holidays
- Help with in-laws at Christmas
- Christmas budget
- Kid Christmas events

Be sure the site includes a welcome video, ways they can share the event with others, social media integration, dates and times of the event as well as a link to your main church website.

For example, The Crossing in Chesterfield, Mo., had 21 services over three campuses, and they created a mini-website to promote the Christmas services.

4. Social Media

Use Facebook, Twitter and Instagram to your advantage. Buy some social media advertising that is directly targeted for your specific audience. Create a profile and cover photo that goes with your series. (The Facebook graphic dimensions cheat sheet might help.) Use Instagram to tell the Christmas story through photos. Design artwork that is easily shared by your attendees. Definitely post these graphics on your church page, and encourage your people to share it. You might even give them directions for how to share.

The Orchard Community in Aurora, Ill., used only social media, word of mouth and their website to promote their five Christmas Eve services. Each one was packed.

5. Community Advertising

Find out what's going on in your community that you can get involved with, have a presence and pass out invites. Find local holiday parades, Christmas light displays and concerts. Find ways to partner with them, advertise at the event or get your foot in the door in other ways. Be creative, and don't be afraid to ask.

AFC Church in Eagle River, Alaska, put on a pajama party for their children's ministry where they got to make homemade ornaments and watch a VeggieTales movie. They also had a photo booth with plenty of Christmas props: antlers, Santa hats, decorated backdrops and naughty/nice signs.

The Fields Church had a float in a local holiday parade and passed out packets of hot chocolate with invite cards on them.

Northside Christian Church in Wadsworth, Ohio, handed out simple, small brown boxes before their services and instructed everyone to wait until communion to open them. Inside was a prepackaged communion wafer and juice. After talking about God's perfect gift, the entire church was able to partake in communion together.

Rockford First in Rockford, Ill., advertised their Christmas service with 30-second radio spots and posted signs on the side of the road.

Pure Heart in Glendale, Ariz., trucked in 50 tons of snow for the kids to play in on Christmas Eve weekend. It was probably the first white Christmas some those kids had ever had before.

Elevate Church in Morton, Ill., put up two billboards in high traffic locations and had volunteers post invites—with mini disco balls attached—to public bulletin boards.

6. Email Marketing

Email is not dead. Email typically gets much higher click-through rates than social media. Your email list should be your congregation. It's a highly targeted list of people already engaged with your church. Reach out to them, point to the ways you're promoting your Christmas services and encourage them to invite their friends.

7. Content Marketing

Ebook

Create an ebook that talks about Christmas. It could be something as simple as fun traditions compiled into one book or something as deep as the true meaning of Christmas. Although an ebook takes a lot of planning and work, it's a great way to get your church's name out into the community and generate anticipation for the Christmas season.

Free Song Download

You could also give away a free download of a Christmas song on your website. It could be a special rendition of a classic by your church choir and a teaser for the music that will be in your Christmas service.

Devotionals

Challenge your congregation to write Advent devotions the few weeks leading up to Christmas. To put a twist on them, have children draw pictures of their favorite part of the Christmas story and post them around the church. You could also involve teens by having them pick out pieces of Scripture and then put these in a book available to the congregation or post them on the church blog. This will get the entire congregation involved.

Anne Marie Miller wrote a book of Advent devotions, *Surviving Christmas: Advent Devotions for the Hard and Holy Holidays*. You can download the book for free. (And stay tuned for an upcoming chapter from Anne.)

8. Videos

There are plenty of free Christmas videos available to churches that you can show before or during a sermon, post to your social media accounts or even use as pre-service entertainment. They're also a great way to keep your congregation's attention, especially during a sermon. You can check out the Church Marketing Sucks website for our favorite Christmas videos.

Rockford First went so far as to create their own 25-minute short film for their annual TV special on local networks.

There are tons more videos at your disposal. Just be careful of copyright laws—some videos are freely available to share with your congregations, but you might have to buy others in order to share.

Evan Courtney is an executive pastor in the middle of the Illinois cornfields at The Fields Church. He owns a creative design company, Creative Courtney, and is a Creative Missions alumni.

Web: EvanCourtney.com
Twitter: @EvanCourtney

"On Dec. 5, we're going to start the 12 days of serving, and we're going to serve our community for 12 days during Christmas. We couldn't think of a better way to express the true heart of Christmas."

Stephen Brewster
creative arts pastor
Cross Point Church

10 Ways Your Church Can Have a Social Media Christmas

by Paul Prins

Let's face it, we have a hard time getting people to show up 10 minutes early to the church service to shake hands and greet people. Yet we hope they will engage in a meaningful way with us online. Christmas is a busy time of year for those of us working at churches and for everyone in our community.

With that in mind, **here are 10 easy ways to engage people on social media this Christmas/Advent season:**

1. Caption Contest

The main idea here is to highlight a specific moment in the Christmas story. There have been a lot of historic paintings, photography and other artwork done on the subject. All you need to do is find an image, add a word or thought bubble, and provide a bit of context. Set the scene, and let people leave their best caption.

Possible Moments:

- Mary's initial response or first thought after being told she's pregnant.

- Joseph's first words after Mary tells him she's with child.
- If Joseph asked the angel one question to prove its angelic-ness, what would it be?

2. Re-Enact a Scene

This one is great for families. Encourage people to stage a scene from the story at home. If you put a bit of thought into it ahead of time, you might be able to get many families to do different parts of the same story. Those images can be used online and/or during the slides on Sunday. The idea is to have fun and let kids be kids.

Possible Moments:

- Pretending to be pregnant (because kids stuffing pillows in their shirts is always funny).
- Being turned away from the inn.
- The magi arriving with presents.
- Fleeing to Egypt.

3. Photo Booth & Selfie Station

Take a bit of time to collect some Christmas-related props for a photo booth in the foyer. After the service, encourage people to go back to the booth, grab some props and take a fun photo to share online. Ideally, you would have a staff member or volunteer encouraging people to get their photo taken. This person could take pictures for others with their phones for them to share and possibly with a camera for the church. That way, people can share their pics with their friends while you can also put an album online of everyone's photos.

Prop Ideas: White beards; Santa hats; shepherd hats and staff/cane; magi robes/wraps; plastic animal masks (from the stable); fake/real gold; frankincense with a name tag for "Frank" plus a bundle of incense to go with the name tag; myrrh; "No Vacancy" sign; halos; etc.

4. If You Were _____

If you were the innkeeper and Mary and Joseph came to your full house, where would you put them up? If you were the magi, what gift would you bring? The goal is to engage people with the Christmas story. Encourage them to go take a picture to illustrate their idea (the garage where you'd let Mary and Joseph stay, the Xbox you'd bring as a gift, etc.). The hope is to connect people with a story they have heard a hundred times in a new way.

Ideas:

- Innkeeper – Where would you put Mary and Joseph?
- Magi – What precious gift would you bring Jesus? (Great to ask kids.)
- Shepherd – How would you respond to an-

gels showing up in the middle of the night?

5. Your Best Unexpected Present

It's easy to forget that no one expected what Jesus was to become—a Savior who willingly died for us. He was an unexpected Savior in so many ways, being what we needed in ways that surpassed our desires. Some people understood who Jesus was, but they had no idea what that would ultimately mean. The idea here is to encourage people to think back on their most unexpected Christmas present and share it in words or a picture.

6. Make a Manger Contest

A manger is basically a feeding trough for animals. What would make a good manger today? Laundry basket? Dresser drawer? Pose a challenge for people in your church community to make their version of a manger from odds and ends they find around the house. Ideally, they shouldn't take more than a few minutes putting something together. Bonus points if they have a doll, stuffed animal or an actual baby in their picture for scale.

Have people share these pictures online (either on your Facebook page or use a hashtag on Twitter) so you can collect them. Award a prize the next Sunday for the most creative manger. My personal recommendation is for the prize to be a bunch of hay or a bag full of myrrh.

7. Share Your Census Journey

Mary and Joseph had to travel to Bethlehem for the census. While this is no longer a thing (thank goodness), you can help people imagine what that would be like. Have everyone use Google Maps to find the walking directions from your church or their house to the town they grew up in. Have them share the name of their hometown and how many hours that journey would be.

This can get challenging for folks born across an ocean—Google's walking directions don't include swimming. But you can get close by getting walking directions to a major coastal city on both ends with flight directions in between. For example: walking directions from Ohio to New York City, then a flight to Lisbon, Portugal, then walking directions to Addis Ababa, Ethiopia. (FYI, it's almost 1,700 hours, plus a 7-hour flight, and includes a ferry—that's at least a 70-day journey.)

8. Breaking the News

If you didn't know, the Bible is a bit of a shorthand version of what happened. Not every conversation was documented. So have some fun imagining how they broke the news to other people in the story. This is like the caption contest idea, but focused on starting a difficult conversation. Plus, the brainstorming might help people with upcoming awkward family conversations that might happen over the holidays.

News to Break:

- Mary shares with Joseph that she's pregnant.
- Joseph informs his parents about Mary.
- Shepherd tells his friends an angel showed up.
- The magi propose a long road trip based on a star.

9. #ThrowbackChristmas

We've seen how fun Throwback Thursday can be, so how about Throwback Christmas? Start a post online asking people to post old Christmas photos, pictures of their favorite gift or share a favorite Christmas memory. Hopefully, it generates nostalgia, good memories and awkward childhood photos. It'll work best if you get the ball rolling with some of the staff sharing their own throwbacks.

10. Your Pet as a Christmas Character

People love pets. If someone has pets, it is guaranteed they will have pet photos on their phone. The idea is pretty simple: get people to post a picture of their pet and place them in the Christmas story as a character. It's even more fun when people get creative with different characters in the Christmas story. Not everyone's cockatoo can be Joseph. I imagine my cat as the innkeeper and my dog as the bellhop at the inn. Maybe your hamster is powering the "No Vacancy" sign.

Paul Prins is the founder of Fresh Vine membership software and a pastor and church planter with Christian Associates. He loves the local church and all the ways that he gets to participate in what God is doing in the world.

Web: freshvine.co
Twitter: @PaulPrins

"In all of your planning, in all of your preparation, keep Jesus as the central thing—communicating the gospel, communicating the love of Christ. Don't come up with these big elements just for the sake of being creative."

Wade Joye
worship pastor
Elevation Church

Christmas Communication Lessons From Last Year

by Karen Shay-Kubiak

Like most churches, we're always looking for new ways to make our Christmas services the best they can be. Since some of the best learning comes from looking back, I thought I'd share a few Christmas communication lessons from last year.

Backstory First

Elmbrook Church is a single-campus megachurch, with an average weekend attendance between 4,500 and 5,000.

At Christmas, we typically see about 10,000 individuals come through our doors, **many of whom have little to no affiliation with a home church**. For that reason, we view Christmas as a prime opportunity to appeal to newcomers.

We faced two unique challenges last year. One was that we were seven months into a 15-month gap between senior pastors. Our congregation had mixed levels of commitment to the church. Many were in a "wait and see" mode.

The second challenge, related to the first, was that

giving was down considerably from the prior year. We made budget cuts in many places to match giving. As a result, the promotion budget was cut in half. **I was committed to doing more with less**.

Our communication team's objective was to do what we could to keep Christmas attendance at or above that of previous years. **We accomplished this**—with help from the Holy Spirit! Estimated attendance was about the same as the year before. We celebrated this as a small victory.

We Kept What Worked in Previous Years

- An event page on the website (with a simple URL we used in all promotions).
- Ads in community newspapers' church directories the week before.
- A large road sign containing service times on a high-visibility section of our property.
- An all-church email from the interim senior pastor to our email list of more than 11,600, encouraging them to pick up invitations and envelopes in the coming weekends and invite a friend.
- A small giveaway for attendees.
- Facebook event page.
- Facebook posts promoting Christmas Eve, including photo images.
- Twitter posts that were basically repurposed Facebook posts.

I did not do any additional advertising in the community, such as Christmas cards mailed to local residents, yard signs, a billboard or any of the other more costly things we had done in the past.

We Added Some New Tactics

- I added a social media "how to" section to the website event page to make it invitation-friendly.
- We stuffed invitation cards into bulletins three weeks prior. We had envelopes available that people could use to mail the invitations. We left room in the design for a personal note.
- I sent an email to staff explaining how to share on Facebook and how to invite friends to Christmas services via social media.
- Our café printed coffee sleeves that promoted Christmas with "invite a friend" and the URL on them.
- I added images to the website created specifically to be shared on Pinterest, which included the URL for the event in the image.
- I ran a Facebook-promoted post about Christmas Eve services, driving people to the website event page. With Facebook's targeting abilities, I selected that the ad only be shown to those who were not already fans of the church and who lived within a 15-mile radius. It cost about $175 to get in

the news feed of thousands of individuals in our community. I paid per click on the ad, so I knew they made it to our web page.

The Results

- There were 4,931 visitors to our website event page. Of those, 1,271 landed there directly via the event URL.
- There were over 1,500 social shares of the website event page. This means these folks were on the event page and shared it via the sharing icons at the top of the page.
- As already stated, attendance was on par with the prior year. Objective met!

Lessons Learned

A number of people told me that the social media "how to" on the event page was helpful. I've leveraged this concept since then in other situations where I want folks to support our social media efforts.

Apparently, many people are not confident navigating the brave new world of social media without a little guidance.

Not surprisingly, **the Facebook posts with images got much better engagement than posts without**. I've increased our mix of image posts on Facebook throughout the year. This has made a big difference in boosting audience engagement.

Doing Things Differently This Year

I plan to be more strategic with Pinterest and Facebook images, creating several in advance and scheduling them to post periodically so fans start to expect them from us on a regular basis.

Based on feedback, I realized that we have two audiences coming to the website event page, and only a portion of them resonate with the "invite a friend" message. So I am going to move the invitation and "how to" to a separate page. That way, **newcomers won't have to wade through that information to get the nuts-and-bolts of what they want to know**.

I will spend time sprucing up the content on the "I'm New" and "Weekends at Elmbrook" web pages, which were the pages people visited immediately after the Christmas page.

I am also adding links to the Christmas page on all other holiday event pages, such as our women's Christmas celebration and the holiday ballet performance.

Karen Shay-Kubiak is director of communications for Elmbrook Church, a single-campus megachurch located in Southeast Wisconsin. She blogs about church communications, food struggles and wandering in the woods at KarenShayKubiak.com.

Web: KarenShayKubiak.com
Twitter: @KShayKubiak

"If you could do nothing else but read from the Gospel of Luke, you would be communicating the greatest story of all."

Shawn Wood
lead pastor
Freedom Church

13 Last-Minute Christmas Ideas

by Robert Carnes

We're all familiar with last-minute Christmas shopping. I'm one of the worst when it comes to Yuletide procrastination. Some of us don't even start buying gifts until Christmas Eve.

However, last minute is not a good policy when it comes to Christmas planning at your church. It takes a good deal more time to successfully orchestrate church events than it does to pick up some tacky sweaters from the department store.

If you've waited until a month before Christmas to start planning, you're in for a rough ride. That's not enough time to build a Christmas campaign from scratch. (Well, maybe a small campaign, if you like long hours and stress, which we do not endorse.) It is, however, plenty of time to get the word out about said Christmas campaign. It's even enough time to add a little more to your Christmas promotion.

Here are 13 last-minute ideas to promote your church's Christmas events and services:

1. Just like we decorate our homes for the holidays, **give your social media accounts a holiday makeover**. Change out profile or

...os to ones consistent with your
... theme. Or even just add snow-
...anta hats.

...g original content to your social
...ounts daily to serve as a continued
... that the holiday season is upon us.
It could be as simple as quoting appropriate
Bible passages leading up to Christmas.

3. **Create a Christmas promo video**. OK, that sounds like a lot of work, right? It doesn't have to be. Consider ways to make short videos. Use a single camera to record your pastor inviting people to your Christmas services in 30 seconds. Simple.

4. Encourage people to **share their favorite family traditions on social media.** Collect some of the best ones, and share them during services (with their permission, of course).

5. **Pay for some Facebook ads.** You can closely target your audience and only pay for clicks, so you get more bang for your buck.

6. Create **original social media graphics** with worship times that can be easily downloaded and shared by your church members.

7. Join the Anglican Communion Churches in celebrating Advent with your camera phone.

8. To sweeten the deal, attach invitations to a packet of hot chocolate. We know how effective church visitor gifts can be.

9. **Invite your neighbors**. Make sure your neighborhood knows what's going on at

your church for Christmas—put up yard signs or banners with the dates and times. Then go the extra mile and invite your neighbors personally.

10. The community bulletin board is an overlooked outlet. **Print up fliers, and put them up around town**. Coffee shops, libraries, college campuses—even Jimmy Johns and Panera—have bulletin boards for community notices. Just be sure you get permission first.

11. Community service is a powerful way to show how you care for your community. **Consider adding a service component to your events**. Maybe it's something simple like collecting socks for the homeless at your services. Maybe it's something small that your staff does. Maybe you share about it online to encourage everybody to give back (or maybe you don't—bragging doesn't go over well).

12. **Invite one person yourself**. You're doing all this work to promote your church's Christmas services and encourage your congregation to invite people. Who have you invited? Take a moment to think of someone and invite them. Call them up, send them an email, write them a note.

13. So you get all these people to come to your Christmas service. **What next?** You got them in the door, now how are you going to get them to come back? Think about what

you're going to do after Christmas and how you can bring those visitors back.

Robert Carnes is the marketing and communications manager at Make-A-Wish Georgia. Previously, he worked in communications at two United Methodist churches in Metro Atlanta and also helps out as the assistant editor of Church Marketing Sucks.

Web: jamrobcar.com
Twitter: @jamrobcar

"What happens in most churches in America, people come in for the Christmas programs, the Christmas Eve services, and they really enjoy what they see and have a great experience, but then they leave. And we never hear from them again."

Maurilio Amorim
president/CEO
The A Group

Welcoming Visitors During & After Christmas

by Jonathan Malm

I was always a shepherd when it came to Christmas plays at church. Of course, I wanted to be someone more important, like an angel or Joseph, but for some reason I always got a shepherd. I'm not sure if it was because I lacked the acting talent or if my mom already had the costume, so she forced me into it. Regardless, each year I'd get on stage with my shepherd stick and do my best to act shepherd-y in front of the whole church.

If you grew up in an old-school church, I'm sure your experience was somewhat similar to mine. Some of you might have had cotton sheep on stage with you, some of you had real animals and some of you had a new mother in the congregation brave enough to lend her newborn baby to the production. That's just what we did.

Historically, Christmas is where we do something different. We never have live-action plays on stage during the rest of the year, but Christmas is an opportunity to change things up. It's a break from the boring norm—both for guests and for the regulars. It's the most exciting time of the year because church is, well, boring the rest of the time.

I'm glad to say that has changed over the years. Our church services are getting more engaging. The quality of music is improving. The relevance of the message to people's lives is at an all-time high. Christmas no longer has to be the most exciting time of the year because we're trying to make each service as exciting as possible.

But we still do Christmas differently. We still pull out the cantatas, the plays or "specials" for Christmas. It's just tradition that we do something different on Christmas.

The problem is that those folks who only visit on Easter and Christmas only get to see different stuff on Easter and Christmas. They don't get a chance to see what church is really like because we're always doing something different during those seasons.

If we want guests to come back after visiting the first time, why would we do something different? Wouldn't we want to show them what they could expect next week if they chose to return?

I'm not saying nix the Christmas songs. I'm not saying get rid of the special Christmas reading. But I am saying that what you do on Christmas should feel like your church's unique DNA. People should see your church's personality precisely—only Christmas-themed.

That's the first way to get Christmas guests to come back the rest of the year—let them know what they'll be coming back to. But for many guests, that's not enough. You have to remember: many of the people attending your Christmas services were dragged there by parents or attended out of a sense of guilt. Showing them church isn't that bad is the first step, but there needs to be more.

What many churches do is plan one of their most interesting sermon series to start right after the Christmas or Easter church service. Give them a topic they have already been curious about, then show how you will uniquely answer their questions. Some of the topics people constantly struggle with are:

- Relationships
- Finances
- Controversies in the church and politics

Discover a felt need in your community, and speak to it in a series after your big event. Note: I said felt need, not necessarily a real need. The truth is that everyone needs Jesus. Everyone needs to learn to pray more. Everyone needs to learn to love more. But those aren't necessarily what your community's felt needs are. We don't always think we need what we actually need. And what we think we need isn't necessarily what we really need.

Think of a kid who "needs" that new toy for

Christmas. The truth is that when he gets the toy, he'll probably just put it aside in a few minutes and play with the box it came in. But tempting a kid at Christmas with a cardboard box just won't cut it. It's the same with tempting your guests to come back after Christmas.

So develop a high-impact series, and pour some serious time into promoting it during your Christmas services. Even offer them a small taste of what's coming to whet their appetite.

Just be sure you give people a little bit of slack since the next couple of Sundays after Christmas usually involve travel for people. You can count on people vacationing during holidays. Thus, you also need to find a way to remind people after they get back from their trips that something good is happening at your church that next Sunday.

Basically, put good effort into planning your Christmas services. But put even better effort—programming, marketing, series planning—into the weeks after Christmas. Sometimes we put all our effort into planning Christmas, knowing we're having visitors, and we wear ourselves out. But we know people are going to visit for Christmas, even if we didn't market the services that much. Why not tell those visitors you're putting just as much, if not more, effort into the next series that you want them to return for?

To be honest, Christmas is fairly easy. It's traditional elements. Don't wear yourself out on that stuff. Why not focus your energy on getting guests to return?

Jonathan Malm is a creative entrepreneur and writer. He is the author of *Created for More* (Moody, 2014), a 30-day devotional to help you develop a more creative mind, and *Unwelcome* (CFCC, 2014), a book about making first-time guests feel more welcome at your church.

Web: JonathanMalm.com
Twitter: @JonathanMalm

"At a grand finale, it's easy to find yourself ready to take a bow and accept applause for a job well done. At a grand opening, you are hopeful for what's to come, but you know there is still work to be done and you have to have faith. When you are tempted to pat yourself on the back after hitting a record attendance number this Christmas, try to remember that your work has just begun."

Kathryn Binkley
founder
Alyght Communications

Over-Christmased

The Treason of the Season: Stop the Stress

by Kevin D. Hendricks

Do you hear what I hear? It's the sound of stressed out church communicators grinding their teeth. December places us in the midst of the frenzied holiday season. It can be especially hectic at church as you're preparing for one of the biggest events of the year.

So rather than wait until Dec. 26, now is a good time to stare down the stress. Whether you're a lone volunteer or the leader of a team, you need to take action to restore sanity.

Remember Gratitude

It's easy to forget to give thanks while we're still eating Thanksgiving leftovers. Take some time to push back from your computer and reflect on all you have to be thankful for. Make a list if you need to (and check it twice, because it's not a to-do list). Then express that gratitude. Write some thank you notes. Call up a friend. Send an email that's not asking for anything.

Take some time to remember what you love about this job, and revel in it. Tell your boss thank you.

Spend some time with God in prayer, reflecting on your work, your stress, your challenges and your joys. Say thank you to God.

Give the Gift of Thanks

Say thank you to the many people who make communication happen at your church with an unexpected gift. You may not have a budget to pay volunteers, but you should be able to scrape together a few bucks for a small gift. Maybe it's something fun like *Temptation Bangs Forever: The Worst Church Signs You've Ever Seen* or something practical like a gift card for a local coffee shop. Maybe it's something fun for the office, like Nerf guns or one of those crazy remote-controlled helicopters. Or maybe it's something made with love, like some homemade Christmas cookies.

Even if you work alone, you likely have people you rely on, whether it's the Facebook friend who offers advice or the pastor who oversees your work. Find a way to give something back to show how much you appreciate them.

Give to Yourself

While the holiday season is all about others, it's OK to think about yourself. Take a break at the coffee shop, get yourself a treat and spend some time by yourself. Don't bring your work with you.

Or get yourself a gift this year. Buy that book you've been dying to read, or splurge on some new music. Get yourself something that can help you handle the stress, whether it's a box of Legos or a night at the movies.

Refresh

It's hard to take time to reflect and refresh when we're facing a deadline, but doesn't it sound nice? Make a plan to do it. Register for a conference next year, or add a good book to your wishlist. Schedule some time to step back and rediscover your inspiration and passion.

Maybe the week between Christmas and New Year's is a good time for reading. Pick something motivational, perhaps our own *Church Communication Heroes Volume 1* or maybe Addie Zierman's *When We Were On Fire: A Memoir of Consuming Faith, Tangled Love and Starting Over*. You don't have to read something super practical, but find a good read that can help you think about how we talk about our faith.

Maybe it's time to plan a party for your team. Put a game night on the calendar, or plan a "Christmas is over!" party for the middle of January. Make sure your team has a chance to recharge.

Or maybe put that spring or summer event on the calendar now so you know you have a refreshing break coming up. Pulling the trigger on these events is always hard, especially if the budget is tight or non-existent. But now is the time to do it. Request the budget. Start saving your pennies. The longer you put it off, the more likely you'll forget, and soon it's too late.

Stop Stress Sooner

Christmas is a good time to remember gratitude, but it's kind of a last-ditch effort. Do it now to help yourself and your team. But next year don't wait until everyone is stressed. Make a plan to do something throughout the year, whether it's taking your volunteers out for coffee or sending thank you notes.

Kevin D. Hendricks is the editor of Church Marketing Sucks and editorial director for the Center for Church Communication. He's a freelance writer and editor in St. Paul, Minn., and likes to read a lot—he wrote *137 Books in One Year: How to Fall in Love With Reading*.

Web: KevinDHendricks.com
Twitter: @KevinHendricks

"This Christmas, one of the best gifts you can give yourself and others is the gift of honesty. Be yourself. Be honest."

Broderick Greer
curate
Grace-St. Luke's Episcopal Church

Hospitalized by Christmas

by Anne Marie Miller

In the first Christmas pageant I remember, I played Joseph. Not an angel. Not even Mary.

Joseph.

My family lived in a very small, very rural town in West Texas where my dad was the pastor. There weren't many kids in our church and, evidently, not enough boys to act as Joseph. With my mascara beard and long robe, I carried a stick of wood up to the manger scene where Mary and baby Jesus were.

Twenty years later, I wasn't an angel or Mary or Joseph, and there actually wasn't a Christmas play like my former childhood years. Instead, I was the creative director at a church of 3,000 in the Midwest, and I was producing 10 services a weekend. At Christmas, I think we had 15.

From organizing hundreds of volunteers to getting the stage set, to seeing the website updated and marketing our Christmas program across our city, to interacting with media and convincing people to avoid spending time with their families and instead sit behind a soundboard for five hours twice a day all Christmas weekend long—Christmas wasn't about celebrating anything. In fact, I was looking forward to celebrating my first day off in a month after the "festivities" slowed down.

The fast-paced environment of that church and my inability to create boundaries even in small ways eventually sent me to a hospital—yes, literally. And all because my body could no longer handle the stress—*the stress of celebrating Christ's birth with his church.*

Does something seem a little off to you about that statement? Let me repeat:

I spent a week in the hospital due to the stress I allowed in my life from serving in a church.

I don't want to point fingers at the church. No, I accept complete responsibility for my actions—my eating habits, my late nights and my excessive intake of caffeine. But it's so easy to get caught up in the "spirit of the season" that it just becomes the "stress of the season," and we lose sight of what's truly important.

A few years later, I left my vocation of working in full-time church ministry. I chose to go to a liturgical, Anglican church for several years. No lights. No show. Even though Advent is an incredibly sacred season, the pace of the church doesn't change. It was only when I stepped away from the "stress of the season" that I relearned the beauty and miraculous wonder of it.

I'm not saying everyone needs to take a break from serving their churches or quit their jobs when it's stressful. The bottom line isn't about where you serve—it's about how you serve.

Are you serving out of abundance, or are you running on fumes?

The only way to serve out of abundance is to be empty. I certainly felt depleted during those stressful Christmases. But there's a difference between empty and depleted.

When you're empty, you've intentionally allowed yourself to surrender to God and his work in you, knowing that the biggest work of all—Christ was born, Christ died, Christ was risen and Christ will come again—has already happened. You keep your focus poured into your communion with God. You remove distractions, coping mechanisms and escaping.

In a way, you fast. You fast from the "producing" mentality so many of us carry, and replace it with the "receiving" mentality Christ wants us to have. As you empty, you are filled by his grace through you, and that grace naturally overflows to others.

When you're depleted, you have nothing. What you give is the leftovers of your own strength and ego.

It's obligation, and while it's still a worthy sacrifice, God desires so much more for you and from you.

God created time and space, and it never ceases to amaze me what he does with it. The days I'm short on time and choose my to-do list over spending time talking with my Abba are the days when nothing ever seems to get done. Days when I slow down, take time with him—the days when I breathe—I see him work in ways I never expect. And these ways remind me of the miracles found not only in Christmas, but in every single day.

In Isaiah, after the Israelites relied upon Egypt for protection and help, God tells them that "only in returning to me and resting in me will you be saved," (Isaiah. 30:15).

Whether your Egypt is in productivity, affirmation from others or even in trying to prove something to yourself—as you find yourself growing weary, remember his words. He is waiting for you to come to him. And he is faithful.

> "So the LORD must wait for you to come to him, so he can show you his love and compassion. For the LORD is a faithful God. Blessed are those who wait for his help." (Isaiah 30:18)

Anne Marie Miller is the author of four books and

speaks at colleges, conventions, and churches on the topics of social justice, sexuality, health, addiction, and biblical themes of grace and restoration. She also writes for various publications, studied family sociology and is currently pursuing her DMS at Rockbridge Seminary.

Web: AnneMarieMiller.com
Twitter: @GirlNamedAnne

"Try not to offer so many service opportunities and giving opportunities and projects and programs and shows and different things for your people to do this season that they actually miss the true message of Christmas. … In this economy, we want our people to understand that you don't have to spend a lot of money to make Christmas special."

Bethany Russell
communications director
Christ Fellowship

For the Love of God, Rethink Christmas

by Josh Cody

At the end of 2008, we approached the Christmas season with trepidation as the economy slowed to a crawl. No less than the *New York Times* reported on how churches were responding, including one instance that struck me as ridiculous: An archbishop gave churches "some pastoral insights and suggestions about how we might prepare to celebrate Christmas this year when economic conditions are so grim."

At first glance, it seems benign. A second glance, however, reveals a deep, deep issue. How far off do we have to be if the celebration of a baby born in dirt and straw can be impacted by economic conditions?

I think Jesus would be heartbroken (or even angry) that churches so often remain silent on the frivolity of Black Friday or a fully-stocked living room on Christmas morning while so many are in such desperate need.

Sometimes, **I worry that we're more committed to Santa Claus than Christ himself around this time of year**.

Real World Examples

A story to illustrate my point—recently, at a local church Christmas production, the show climaxed with Santa Claus coming out in a sleigh with presents to sing a little ditty about how Jesus is the reason for the season.

Sorry Santa, but you sit on a throne of lies. If Jesus were still the reason for the season, you'd be out of business.

A different church I attended lamented the woes of taking the capital C out of Christmas. Unfortunately, my experience shows that you're 76 times more likely to find a church out causing a ruckus because someone said "Happy holidays" instead of "Merry Christmas" than you are to find a church causing a ruckus because this annual rat race is ending with people trampled on the floor of Wal-Mart.

Even *The Boston Globe* can spot the disturbing truth: "On this Black Friday in Long Island, consumerism looked more like modern idolatry."

The Solution?

Here's what I believe churches should be doing around Christmas in the midst of a down-turn, and it's pretty simple: Redefine Christmas.

Initiatives like Advent Conspiracy are making headway, but more needs to be done. There is a problem, and it's deep. It's not just personal or societal or cultural. It's a pandemic. People are born with sin, and marketers all too often use that sin to make a buck. That's where church marketers come in.

We have the task of communicating the tough message that so much of this Christmas we have built is a lie. We can try to explain Santa Claus, Christmas trees, gift-giving, candy canes and reindeer poop as Christian traditions, one rung below the sacraments on the ladder of righteousness.

(One aside: I have to give a hat tip to churches who are successfully moving toward this already. Operation Christmas Child, Angel Food Ministries and Angel Tree come to mind.)

There's a harsh reality that the 15 pounds we gain between Thanksgiving and New Year's comprise enough food to save many, many lives. And the old clothes we throw out to make way for the new could clothe the homeless on those cold, winter nights. When we support the Christmas craze—implicitly or explicitly—we communicate that we don't care.

Practical Ideas

Here are my humble ideas for what your church ought to be doing. I'll start with the most radical and work down to the more realistic:

- **Move Christmas.** Choose a day, and tell your congregation you will take that time to celebrate together what happened in the manger 2,000 years ago. You might still have a candlelight service and tell the Christmas story or observe traditions focused on Christ, but Santa, gifts and blinking lights can have their usual October to December time slot.
- **Stop celebrating Christmas.** Just give it up all together. Challenge your congregation to live the whole year in "the Christmas spirit" and come out against the consumerism of it all. Challenge people not to go in debt for that toy or trinket. If you don't want to stop celebrating, at least challenge them to stop gift giving or only give homemade gifts.
- **Teach Financial Peace University.** Careful planning, saving and spending will allow your congregation to be more generous than ever. Encourage them to give a Financial Peace University course as a gift, or better yet, offer it as a Christmas gift to your congregation. Christmas would be a great time to get out of debt instead of into it.
- **Celebrate the 12 Days of Christmas by serving**. Coordinate a Christmas service project for your church. Give money to someone in the community who has medical expenses and can't celebrate Christmas

so they can have a better chance to celebrate next Christmas together. Clean up a park. Take on 12 projects, and invite everyone to participate as often as possible. Culminate with a big project on Christmas Day in lieu of traditional Christmas morning antics.

- **Preach hope.** At the very least, you should be preaching hope. Hope isn't a friend of fools, so people shouldn't be taking payday loans at 500% interest to cover the cost of their presents. However, they should know that there is a God who wants to save them from this craziness. If you have to use a lame pun in your sermon title, so be it (although I would prefer you not). But there is only one place people can turn for hope, and they need to drive the opposite direction of Wal-Mart for it.

Expect More From Christmas

As the Grinch himself learned, Christmas doesn't come from a store—but it's up to churches to show people that it means a lot more.

So for the love of God, let's rethink Christmas.

Josh Cody served as our associate editor for several years before moving on to bigger things, like Texas. These days he lives in Austin, Texas, with his wife, and you can find him online or on Twitter when he's not wrestling code.

Web: JoshuaCody.net
Twitter: @jpcody

When the song of the
angels is stilled,
When the star in the sky is gone,
When the kings and
princes are home,
When the shepherds are back
with their flock,
The work of Christmas begins:
To find the lost,
To heal the broken,
To feed the hungry,
To release the prisoner,
To rebuild the nations,
To bring peace among brothers,
To make music in the heart.

Howard Thurman
late author, professor and civil rights leader

More

About the Center for Church Communication

We are a firebrand of communicators, sparking churches to communicate the gospel clearly, effectively and without compromise.

We are made up of passionate change agents, experienced communication professionals and thoughtful instigators, advocating for communicators to find their place in the church—and helping the church get through to their communities so that churches know who they are and are unashamed to tell others.

We identify, resource and celebrate the next generation of church communicators, encouraging them to focus their tenacity and talent for excellent communication so that churches are sought out by the communities they serve.

We provide smart coaching and mentoring through social media, publishing, events and one-on-one relationships, spotlighting communication that is true, good and beautiful—prompting others to do the same—so that more outsiders become a part of a church community.

We remove barriers to change the way people see Christians and how they speak about the church by promoting relationships, resources, ideas and models for communication. We collaborate people's gifts/skills to work in concert with the Creator and their local church.

As God's story comes alive to us and others, we see gospel-centered local churches that captivate the attention and liberate the imagination of their community, resulting in more people saying, **"That's what church should be!"**

Center for Church Communication:
Courageous storytellers welcome.

Visit CFCCLabs.org to learn more about our projects and get involved.

For more practical tips, inspiration and stories from fellow communicators, visit our flagship blog, Church Marketing Sucks.

More Church Communication Help
You need all the help you can get when planning for the holidays. Check out these other resources from the Center for Church Communication to get more ideas and inspiration:

Church Christmas Ideas
Find even more ideas, examples and Christmas resources for churches at Church Marketing Sucks.

Easter Book
Are you ready for Easter? Get ideas and strategies for planning and promoting your church's Easter service compiled in one place.

Go to cfcclabs.org/easter to purchase this book.

Unwelcome: 50 Ways Churches Drive Away First-Time Visitors
Jonathan Malm talks about how churches drive away visitors and gives advice for keeping them in the pews.

Go to UnwelcomeBook.com to purchase this book.

Free Social Media Graphic

A picture is worth a thousand words (which is great when it comes to promoting your Christmas series or event). So we're giving you one for free. Use this Christmas graphic to share the joy of the season on social media.

Download the free graphic here:
http://cmsucks.us/aag

If you don't like this graphic, you can always create your own. *The Church Graphics Handbook* has plenty of tips and help.

We hope either of these options help you with your Christmas series or event. Happy planning!

Acknowledgements

Thanks to our contributors: Stephen Brewster, Robert Carnes, Josh Cody, Evan Courtney, DJ Chuang, Katy Dunigan, Kelley Hartnett, Kevin D. Hendricks, Jonathan Malm, Anne Marie Miller, Paul Prins, Karen Shay-Kubiak, Dave Shrein and Darrell Vesterfelt.

Thanks for the quotes: Maurilio Amorim, Kathryn Binkley, Stephen Brewster, Laurie Brock, Neal F. Fischer, Neil Greathouse, Broderick Greer, Wade Joye, Bethany Russell, Chuck Scoggins, Howard Thurman, Haley Veturis and Shawn Wood.

Kevin D. Hendricks for guiding this project and making sure it stayed on track.

Elizabyth Ladwig for compiling and editing all of the content that went into this book.

Sheri Felipe for the festive cover design.

374 Designs for the layout of the print edition.

Chuck Scoggins for getting the Center for Church Communication on board with this project.

Katie Strandlund for helping us market and promote this book. Without you, we would never have reached as many people.

Thanks to those who helped proof this book: Celine Murray and Robert Carnes. You created a list and checked it twice (or a dozen times).

We'd also like to give a nod to Tim Schraeder and Shawn Woods for organizing the Planning Christmas series a few years back, which provided a lot of foundational ideas and quotes for this book.

Thank you to everyone reading this book. We hope it helps you in your efforts to make your church's Christmas celebrations more organized, creative and meaningful. As an added bonus, your purchase supports the work of the Center for Church Communication to help churches communicate better. If you found this book valuable, we hope you'll spread the word.

Made in the USA
Middletown, DE
11 November 2015